100 Ways to Celebrate Holidays

Harper Carr

Paperback ISBN: 978-1-962589-17-8
Copyright 2024

Triple A Press

Table of Contents

Introduction

Are you feeling happy and excited about the holiday festivities?

Or perhaps you're feeling sadness or missing a loved one during this time.

Holidays have a way of touching every part of our emotional spectrum.

At the same time that you feel happiness or excitement about something, it's important to remember that the same event could be a source of difficulty or pain for someone else.

You might have plenty of food on your table, while someone else is struggling to make ends meet.

Your big family reunion during the holidays could be a joyful occasion for you but a lonely time for someone with no one to celebrate with.

Even posing for a picture with your beautiful children might unknowingly trigger feelings of heartache for someone who has faced infertility battles.

Similarly, while you're enjoying time with your friends, someone else could be experiencing their loneliest moments.

During this time, being considerate and compassionate can make such a difference in someone's life. A simple gesture, like reaching out to check on a friend or neighbor, can mean the world to someone who might be feeling isolated.

Sharing what you can, whether it's a warm meal, some of your time, or even kind words, helps create a sense of connection and support.

Small acts of kindness, like sending a holiday card, offering a genuine compliment, or even just listening without judgment, can go a long way in lifting someone's spirits.

I've learned that it's not about grand gestures.

Rather, it's about showing others that they are seen, valued, and cared for. By being mindful and empathetic, we can help make the holidays a little brighter for others.

As we gather to celebrate the holidays, it's a wonderful time to focus on ways we can bring joy to ourselves and those around us.

My heartfelt wish is that you find countless reasons to smile and create beautiful memories during this special time of year.

HOLIDAYS

The holiday season is a time of year that brings a whirlwind of emotions.

From the pure joy of sharing special moments with loved ones to the stress of planning and preparation, the core emotions of love, anxiety, sadness, surprise, fear, excitement, anger, disgust, happiness, and gratitude often surface during this festive period.

Each of these emotions plays an important role in shaping our holiday experiences.

To help us all make the most of the holidays, we'll be sharing 100 simple acts that can help brighten the season for both ourselves and others.

LOVE

The holiday season is the perfect time to express love and care for the people in your life. Whether it's through small gestures or grand acts of kindness, the effort you put into showing love is what truly counts.

Finding ways to uplift others can make the season brighter for everyone around you.

Let's explore twenty practical and heartfelt ways to demonstrate love and connection during this special time of year.

One

Listen Actively
Pay attention when someone is speaking to you, showing that you value their thoughts and feelings.

The holidays can be overwhelming for many. Being a good listener provides an outlet for others to express their worries or frustrations, helping them feel supported.

By simply being there to listen, you give others the space to share what's on their mind without judgment or interruption.

For example, during a conversation with a friend who's sharing something important, put away distractions like your phone, maintain eye contact, and nod or respond thoughtfully to demonstrate that you're truly engaged.

Simple actions like asking follow-up questions or paraphrasing their words can go a long way in making them feel heard and appreciated. Active listening fosters deeper connections and shows genuine care.

Clear communication is essential during the busy holiday season. Listening attentively helps avoid conflicts and ensures everyone is on the same page.

Two

Encourage Others

A simple compliment or a heartfelt "You've got this!" can make someone's day better.

Three

Send a Thoughtful Note or Message

A handwritten card, email, or even a quick text filled with kind words can go a long way in lifting someone's spirits. Let them know you're thinking of them and appreciate their presence in your life.

Four

Offer to Help with Tasks

The holidays can be overwhelming. Offering to lend a hand—whether that's wrapping gifts, running errands, or preparing meals—can be incredibly encouraging for someone feeling stressed or exhausted.

Five

Reminisce About Good Times

Share a happy memory you've had together. Reflecting on joyous moments can bring a smile to someone's face and remind them of the positive connections in their life.

Six

Give a Small, Meaningful Gift

If you can afford to, please give a gift. A thoughtful present doesn't have to be extravagant. A homemade treat, a book you know they'd love, or even a cozy blanket can show that you care and brighten their day.

Seven

Offer Words of Affirmation

Tell them how much you admire their strengths or accomplishments. A little recognition can go a long way in boosting confidence, especially during a time when emotions may run high.

Eight

Invite Them to Spend Time Together

Whether it's a casual meet-up, a video call, or a holiday movie night, spending quality time together can remind someone they're not alone and that they're cared for.

Nine

Spread Positivity Where You Can

Whether it's sharing an uplifting quote, cracking a funny joke, or simply having a cheerful attitude, spreading positivity can rub off on others and lift their spirits during the holiday season.

Ten

Spend quality time together - One of the best ways to show love during the holidays is by spending quality time together. Whether it's a long conversation or a fun activity, it's important to be fully present.

This could mean sitting down for a long, meaningful conversation over a cup of hot chocolate, sharing stories, and catching up on each other's lives.

You can also plan fun activities, like baking cookies as a family, decorating the house together, or playing board games that bring everyone together around the table.

For those who enjoy the outdoors, taking a walk or going skating can create special memories.

What matters most is being fully present.

Putting away distractions like phones or work so you can focus on truly connecting with the people you care about. These moments of togetherness leave a lasting impression and deepens bonds.

I remember one New Year's Day when my dad and I spent hours driving together. We sang some of my favorite childhood songs and hymns, filling the car with laughter and music.

As I drove, we reminisced about moments while admiring the buildings and cars we passed. Now that my dad has lost his vision, those memories feel even more precious. I realize now how much I took those simple, beautiful times for granted.

Eleven

Express gratitude - One of the simplest and most heartfelt ways to show gratitude during the holidays is by expressing it directly. Take the time to say "thank you" for the little things. Whether it's for a thoughtful gesture, a shared moment, or simply someone's presence in your life. These words, though small, carry a lot of weight and can make the other person feel deeply appreciated and valued.

You can personalize your thanks by mentioning specific actions or qualities you're grateful for, such as, "Thank you for always being there to listen," or "I'm so grateful for the effort you've put into making this season special." Pairing your words with a handwritten note can amplify the impact.

Twelve

Give thoughtful gifts - It doesn't have to be expensive; something personal and meaningful can show how much you care.

Giving thoughtful gifts during the holidays is a beautiful way to show love and care. To make your gift meaningful, think about the recipient's interests, hobbies, and needs.

Personalized items, such as a photo book filled with shared memories or a handmade craft, can show that you went the extra mile. Even practical gifts, like a cozy blanket for someone who values comfort or a gourmet food basket for a foodie, can bring moments of joy.

Pay attention to conversations in the months leading up to the holidays—people often drop hints about things they'd love without even realizing it.

Most importantly, the act of giving with genuine thought and care matters more than the actual price of the gift. It's the love and effort behind the gesture that truly makes it special.

For example, I loved receiving homemade cards from my son when he was younger. It wasn't about the price of the gift, it was the thought and effort.

Thirteen

Perform acts of service - The holiday season is a perfect opportunity to spread kindness and bring smiles to others. Help someone out by lending a hand, whether it's doing a chore or running an errand for them.

Offer to shovel snow, hang decorations, or pick up groceries for an elderly or busy neighbor. Taking the time to lend a hand shows thoughtfulness and care.

Fourteen

Volunteer at a Local Shelter

Many shelters and food banks need extra hands around the holidays. You could help serve meals, organize donations, or simply spend time with those in need. Your presence and willingness to give back can make all the difference.

Fifteen

Prepare and Deliver Gift Baskets

Create thoughtful gift baskets filled with items like warm socks, snacks, and small holiday treats. These can be given to neighbors, coworkers, or even strangers who might need some extra cheer.

Sixteen

Write Holiday Cards

A heartfelt card can go a long way in lifting someone's spirits. Take time to write personalized holiday cards to friends, family, or even residents at senior living facilities to brighten their day.

Seventeen

Donate to a Holiday Toy Drive

You can help spread joy to children by donating toys to a local toy drive or charity. This simple gesture ensures that every child has something to smile about on holiday mornings.

Eighteen

Show up without being asked

Be there in their moments of need or joy to show that you're thinking of them. Sometimes, the greatest gift you can give someone during the holidays is your time and assistance. Whether it's helping an overwhelmed friend with wrapping gifts, running errands for a busy family member, or offering to babysit so they can have a moment to themselves, these thoughtful gestures can make a lasting impact.

Nineteen

Check-In Regularly - For those who may be feeling lonely or stressed, a simple check-in can mean the world. Send a text, make a phone call, or drop by with a warm drink and a listening ear. Knowing someone is thinking of them can brighten their day.

Twenty

Random Acts of Kindness

Challenge your friends or family to a day of small, kind gestures. Each person can do things like pay for a stranger's coffee, leave a thank-you note for a mail carrier, or shovel a neighbor's driveway. The collective spirit of kindness will warm everyone's hearts.

ANXIETY

The holiday season can be a joyful time, but it also comes with its fair share of stress and anxiety. It's okay to feel overwhelmed, but there are many ways to help ease that tension and enjoy the season to its fullest. The next ten ideas may help you manage anxiety during the holidays.

Twenty One

Plan Ahead

Creating a schedule for events, shopping, and other holiday tasks can reduce the last-minute scramble and bring a sense of control. Even something as simple as making a to-do list can help you stay focused and minimize stress.

Twenty Two

Set Realistic Expectations

Accept that things might not go exactly as planned, and that's okay. Focus on enjoying the moments rather than achieving perfection.

Twenty Three

Say No When Needed

It's easy to feel overwhelmed when you're trying to please everyone. Know your limits and don't be afraid to politely decline invitations or tasks that feel like too much.

Twenty Four

Practice Deep Breathing or Meditation

Taking a few minutes each day to practice deep breathing or mindfulness can help calm your mind and lower stress levels. Apps and guided meditations can be great tools to start this practice.

Twenty Five

Stick to a Budget

Financial stress is a common source of holiday anxiety. Decide on a budget for gifts, decorations, and activities early on, and stick to it. Heartfelt, thoughtful gifts don't have to be expensive!

Twenty Six

Prioritize Self-Care

Don't forget to take care of yourself. Make time for activities that relax you, such as reading, taking a walk, or enjoying a cup of tea. Self-care is not selfish. It's necessary.

Twenty Seven

Limit Holiday Obligations

It's tempting to cram in every party, tradition, and activity, but overcommitting can take a toll on your mental health. Choose the ones that matter most to you and your loved ones.

Twenty Eight

Get Moving

Physical activity can do wonders for anxiety. Whether it's a brisk walk in the fresh air, yoga, or dancing to your favorite holiday songs, exercise releases endorphins that improve your mood.

Twenty Nine

Stay Connected

Reach out to friends or family members when you need support. Holidays are about connection, so don't hesitate to lean on your loved ones if you're feeling overwhelmed.

Thirty

Focus on Gratitude

Take time to appreciate the positive things in your life. Keeping a gratitude journal or simply reflecting on what you're thankful for can shift your mindset and reduce stress.

SADNESS

Dealing with sadness can feel overwhelming, but it's important to remember that there are practical and helpful ways to manage these emotions.

Whether you're supporting yourself or someone else, small, intentional actions can make a big difference. By focusing on self-care, connecting with others, and practicing mindfulness, it's possible to find moments of relief and even build resilience over time.

Below, we'll explore several strategies to help deal with sadness and support those around you who may be struggling, especially during challenging times like the holidays.

Thirty One

Practice Self-Care

Prioritize time for yourself by engaging in activities that bring you comfort and relaxation. This could be as simple as enjoying a warm bath, reading a favorite book, or taking a walk in nature. Self-care allows you to reconnect with yourself and ease feelings of sadness.

Thirty Two

Talk to Someone You Trust

Opening up to a friend, family member, or therapist can help you release difficult emotions. Sometimes, just having someone listen without judgment can bring immense relief and make you feel supported.

Thirty Three

Physical Activity

Physical activity, whether it's dancing, a gentle yoga session or a brisk walk, can boost your mood by releasing endorphins. Exercise has a natural way of reducing stress and lifting spirits, even if it's just for a few minutes each day.

Thirty Four

Journal

Take a moment to reflect on things in your life that bring you joy or fulfillment, no matter how small they seem. Writing these down in a gratitude journal can help shift your perspective and combat persistent sadness over time.

Thirty Five

Allow Yourself to Feel

It's okay to feel sad; don't try to suppress or ignore your emotions. Give yourself permission to process what you're feeling. Crying or expressing your sadness in a healthy way can often be a necessary step toward healing.

Ways to Help Someone Who Feels Sad During the Holidays ...

Thirty Six

Check-In

Reach out and check in with them. Simply being available to hear their thoughts and feelings can make a world of difference. Be patient, empathetic, and avoid trying to "fix" their sadness. Sometimes they just need someone to listen.

Thirty Seven

Encourage Them to Join Activities

Gently invite them to participate in holiday activities like decorating, making festive meals, or watching a holiday movie. Focus on low-pressure activities that allow them to feel included without overwhelming them.

Thirty Eight

Respect Their Feelings

Holidays can be difficult for many reasons, such as missing loved ones or feeling lonely. Show that you understand their emotions and remind them it's okay to feel this way without expecting them to instantly adopt a cheerful demeanor.

Thirty Nine

Give a Thoughtful Gift

A small but meaningful gift, such as a book they'd love, cozy socks, or a handwritten note, can brighten their day and remind them that they are cared for. Personalized gestures often hold a lot of emotional weight.

Forty

Be Present Without Being Overbearing

Sometimes your presence alone can provide comfort. Even if someone doesn't want to talk, simply sitting with them or doing a calming activity together. For example, a puzzle, crafting or knitting can help them feel less isolated during the holidays.

SURPRISE

The holidays are the perfect time to add a little extra magic to the lives of those around us. Small, thoughtful surprises can make a world of difference, turning an already festive season into something even more unforgettable. Here are a few merry ideas.

Forty One

A Surprise Virtual Party

Distance shouldn't prevent holiday celebrations. Organize a virtual holiday party for loved ones, complete with games, music, and themed activities. Send invitations and some goodies in advance to create an exciting build-up.

Forty Two

Holiday Movie Night

Curate a movie night. Include holiday-themed movies, popcorn, cookies, cozy socks, and a blanket to make the evening extra magical.

Forty Three

A Secret Santa Delivery

Prepare a thoughtful gift, wrap it beautifully, and deliver it anonymously. Perhaps it's a cozy sweater, a box of their favorite chocolates, or something they've been eyeing. The mystery behind it adds an extra layer of excitement.

Forty Four

A Secret Santa Delivery

Prepare a thoughtful gift, wrap it beautifully, and deliver it anonymously. Perhaps it's a cozy sweater, a box of their favorite chocolates, or something they've been eyeing. The mystery behind it adds an extra layer of excitement.

Forty Five

Decorate for Someone

If someone you know is too busy or overwhelmed to put up holiday decorations, surprise them by doing it for them! Decking out their home with festive touches can bring instant holiday cheer.

Forty Six

Decorate for Someone

If someone you know is too busy or overwhelmed to put up holiday decorations, surprise them by doing it for them! Decking out their home with festive touches can bring instant holiday cheer.

Forty Seven

DIY Gift Craft Session

Host a craft session where everyone can make their own gifts. Provide all the supplies and guide them through simple projects like ornaments, candles, or photo frames. It's a fun way to create lasting memories and meaningful presents.

Forty Eight

Warm Meal Giveaway

Surprise someone with a home-cooked holiday meal. Whether it's a neighbor, a coworker, or someone going through a tough time, showing up with a warm dish can make them feel loved and remind them of the joy this season brings.

Forty Nine

Surprise Holiday Photoshoot

Arrange a surprise photoshoot for families or friends. Hire a photographer (or do it yourself!) and capture moments surrounded by holiday décor. This creates cherished memories they can look back on for years to come.

Fifty

Caroling

Surprise your neighbors or loved ones with a caroling session. Gather a small group and sing holiday classics from a safe distance. It's a joyful and unexpected way to spread cheer.

FEAR

During the holidays, fear often arises in different forms, depending on individual experiences and circumstances.

For many, there is the fear of financial strain, with the pressure to buy gifts, host gatherings, or travel.

Others may face social fears, such as the anxiety of interacting with distant relatives or attending large festive events.

There can also be a fear of loneliness, particularly for individuals who may not have close family or friends to celebrate with during this time.

Additionally, for those who have experienced loss, the holidays can stir a fear of emotional pain as memories of absent loved ones feel more poignant.

These layers of fear during what is perceived as a joyful season highlight the complexity of emotions tied to holiday traditions and expectations.

Fifty One

Seek Support When Needed

If fear or emotional pain becomes too heavy to handle alone, reach out to a trusted friend, family member, or even a professional counselor. Talking about your emotions can provide relief and may help uncover solutions for navigating the holiday season.

Fifty Two

Create New Traditions

If loneliness or loss is making the holidays intimidating, consider creating new traditions that bring comfort and meaning. Whether it's connecting virtually with others, volunteering, or dedicating time to a hobby, these practices can bring a sense of fulfillment and connection.

Fifty Three

Take Care of Yourself

Social fears, like interacting with distant relatives or attending large gatherings, can feel intimidating. You don't have to attend every party or gathering. Choose events that feel most meaningful and manageable for you.

Self-care is essential, especially when fear starts to take over. Prioritize rest, eat well, and find time for activities that help you relax, like meditation, journaling, or a cozy evening with a book. Taking a moment to breathe deeply or practice mindfulness may help center your emotions.

A calm mind and body are more equipped to manage feelings of fear.

Fifty Four

Shift Your Focus

When fear of something negative happening arises, try to shift your focus to the positive. I know sometimes this could be impossible. But if you are able to, please take a moment each day to reflect on what you're grateful for, whether it's your health, relationships, or small joys. This simple habit may help you create feelings of peace and contentment during a hectic season.

Fifty Five

Budget

Financial stress is a common source of fear
during the holidays. Create a budget that aligns
with your resources. Plan ahead for purchases
or gatherings. This can help you feel more in
control and ease worries about overspending
or running out of resources.

EXCITEMENT

The holiday season is a time to come together, create memories, and celebrate. Whether it's planning a gathering, or simply enjoying the little things like holiday songs or festive lights, there's something undeniably special about the anticipation that comes with this time of year.

Celebrating doesn't have to be grand or perfect. What matters is the moments of joy we create along the way. Here are a few ideas that can get us excited for holidays.

Fifty Six

Plan a Special Holiday Gathering

Take some time to plan a get-together with friends or family. Whether it's an ugly sweater party or a karaoke night, having an event to look forward to can build excitement and make the holidays feel even more meaningful.

Fifty Seven

Create a Holiday Playlist

Music sets the mood! Compile your favorite seasonal songs into a playlist and listen to them as you decorate, wrap gifts, or just relax with a cup of cocoa. Singing or dancing along can instantly lift your spirits.

Fifty Eight

Focus on the Little Joys

The holidays don't have to be extravagant to be meaningful. Focus on small pleasures like cooking your favorite comfort foods, cuddling up with a good book, or enjoying festive decorations around town.

Fifty Nine

Cook or Bake Together

Gather with loved ones in the kitchen and cook or bake something seasonal. Holiday treats fill your home with a nice aroma.

Sixty

Make a Countdown Calendar

Counting down to the big day is half the fun. Whether you use an official calendar or craft your own creative countdown, it adds a sense of anticipation and childlike wonder to the season.

ANGER

Anger has a way of sneaking in during the holidays. Sometimes it's caused by high expectations, misunderstandings, or simply the chaos of holiday preparations.

The good news is that with a little awareness and effort, you can manage your anger and create a more harmonious environment for yourself and those around you.

Whether it's practicing empathy, taking a deep breath, or even just keeping a sense of humor, small actions can make a big difference.

Here are some practical tips to help control your anger or avoid making others upset during the holidays.

Sixty One

Take a Deep Breath

Try to understand the perspectives and feelings of those around you, even if you don't agree with them. When you feel anger rising, pause for a moment and take a few deep breaths to calm yourself before reacting.

Sixty Two

Set Realistic Expectations

The holidays can be stressful, so avoid setting perfectionist expectations for yourself or others. If the holiday chaos gets overwhelming, step away for a moment to regain your composure.

Sixty Three

Communicate Clearly

Misunderstandings often cause frustration. Be clear and polite in expressing your thoughts and needs. Before responding to someone or something provoking, count to ten to give yourself a chance to cool down.

Sixty Four

Know Your Triggers

Reflect on past situations that have made you angry and plan strategies to manage them or avoid them.

Sixty Five

Use "I" Statements

When discussing issues, focus on how you feel instead of blaming others. For example, "I feel upset when..." instead of "You always...".

Sixty Six

Avoid Alcohol Overindulgence

Excess alcohol can amplify emotions, including anger, so drink responsibly.

Sixty Seven

Offer Assistance

Helping out, like setting the table or cooking, can minimize others' stress and diffuse potential tension.

Sixty Eight

Keep Humor Alive

A well-timed joke or lighthearted comment can ease tense situations during family gatherings.

Sixty Nine

Create a Peaceful Atmosphere

Use decorations, scents, or music to set a calming holiday environment. Helping out, like setting the table or cooking, can minimize others' stress and diffuse potential tension.

Seventy

Change the Subject

If a conversation is heading toward conflict, gently redirect it to a lighter or neutral topic.

Seventy One

Get Enough Sleep

Feeling rested can significantly improve your patience and tolerance during busy days.

Seventy Two

Encourage Inclusive Activities

Plan group activities that everyone can enjoy to reduce feelings of exclusion or frustration.

DISGUST

Certain things can spark feelings of disgust even during this festive season. For example, I don't like seeing piles of uneaten food being thrown away. Especially when so many people go hungry!

Then there's the over-commercialization of the holidays. Endless advertisements and pressure to buy unnecessary items.

Crowded shopping malls and chaotic public spaces can also feel overwhelming and unpleasant, especially when people seem to forget common courtesy.

On top of that, some may feel disgusted by excessive decorations or tacky displays that seem more about showing off than spreading genuine cheer.

Here are a few ways to minimize the disgust that we may feel or even how we can avoid making others disgusted.

Ways to Minimize the Feeling of Disgust During the Holidays

Seventy Three

Reduce Food Waste

To combat food waste, plan meals thoughtfully and prepare portions based on the number of guests.

Encourage guests to take leftovers home, or donate excess food to local food banks.

By addressing this issue proactively, you can transform feelings of waste into a sense of purpose.

Seventy Four

Focus on Meaning Over Materialism

The over-commercialization of the holidays can be overwhelming and off-putting. Shift your mindset by focusing on meaningful experiences rather than material possessions.

Consider giving gifts tied to shared memories. Experiences, like spending time with loved ones, often hold more value and help to minimize feelings of resentment toward holiday consumerism.

Seventy Five

Create a Calmer Shopping Experience

Crowded malls and public areas can sometimes spark feelings of disgust or annoyance. Avoid the chaos by shopping early, using online retail options, or visiting stores during quieter hours.

This not only makes holiday shopping more enjoyable but also reduces exposure to stressful and unpleasant environments.

Seventy Six

Appreciate Subtle Decorations

Excessive and overly extravagant holiday decorations often feel ingenuine or overwhelming.

Opt for more simple and tasteful displays, both at home and when engaging in community events, to help minimize the sensory overload.

Seventy Seven

Stay Mindful of Personal Hygiene

Crowded holiday gatherings or events can sometimes magnify an awareness of poor hygiene habits in public spaces, leading to feelings of disgust.

Encourage your immediate family, including yourself, to follow basic cleanliness practices like proper handwashing and tidying shared spaces. A clean environment fosters comfort and positivity.

Ways to Prevent Ourselves from Making Others Feel Disgusted During the Holidays

Seventy Eight

Avoid Over Cluttered Spaces

During holiday gatherings, keep communal areas tidy and free from unnecessary clutter. Guests may feel bothered by overly crowded environments or messy surroundings.

Ensure decorations, gifts, and food stations are well-organized for a more pleasant and welcoming experience.

Seventy Nine

Trim Down the Excess

Flashy and over-the-top holiday displays, whether through decorations or social media posts, can sometimes evoke a negative reaction in others.

Instead, focus on celebrating the season authentically, emphasizing connection over extravagance.

Eighty

Be Thoughtful with Holiday Gifting

Avoid giving gifts that may unintentionally offend or disgust someone, such as items that are overly personal or unappealing to their tastes.

By taking the time to understand what brings joy to the recipient, you can prevent uncomfortable situations and make gift-giving more meaningful.

Eighty One

Practice Kindness in Public Spaces

Whether it's in a crowded mall or while waiting in line, demonstrate common courtesy and patience with others.

Actions like cutting in line or leaving messes behind can create holiday stress and leave others with a negative impression.

HAPPINESS

The Holidays are the perfect opportunity to focus on fostering joy. We can do this through thoughtful gestures, shared traditions, or simple acts of kindness.

We can show that we care, spend quality time with our loved ones, reach out to others who may be feeling lonely, and be considerate of each other.

Here are a few simple but powerful ways to nurture our happiness and well-being during the holidays.

Eighty Two

Decorate Your Home Together

Turn decorating the tree into a family tradition. Get everyone involved by assigning fun tasks, like hanging ornaments, stringing lights, or creating homemade decorations.

Play your favorite holiday music in the background.

This shared activity adds to the festive spirit.

Eighty Three

Cook and Bake

Cooking and baking during the holidays can be a wonderful way to generate joy and create memories. Gather your family or friends in the kitchen and pick a holiday recipe everyone loves. You can even try something new together.

Whether you're decorating cookies, assembling a gingerbread house, or preparing a festive dinner, this activity encourages teamwork, creativity, and plenty of laughter.

Don't worry about perfection; the joy is in the process. Play some holiday music, wear matching aprons, or turn it into a friendly competition to make it even more fun.

Eighty Four

Go on a Light Tour

Walk or drive through neighborhoods or places known for their beautiful holiday decorations. Visiting neighborhoods known for their stunning decorations can be a fun experience for all ages.

Many families and local businesses put effort into creating holiday displays, from string lights to inflatables and themed setups. You can even make it a tradition by inviting friends or family to join you.

Eighty Five

Host a Holiday Craft Night

Invite friends over to create ornaments, wreaths, or holiday decorations.

Set up a cozy space with plenty of supplies like glue guns, ribbons, glitter, and craft paper to get the holiday spirit flowing. You could focus on specific projects or handmade holiday cards.

Don't forget to keep the atmosphere cheerful with festive music, warm drinks like cider, and maybe some holiday treats like cookies or gingerbread. Connecting and celebrating with others during the holidays can be fun.

Eighty Six

Take a Holiday-Themed Photoshoot

Capture the magic of the holiday season with a fun and creative photoshoot. You can start by picking a festive theme. It could be classic holiday charm, a winter wonderland, or something quirky like dressing as your favorite holiday characters.

Matching outfits, like cozy holiday sweaters, pajamas, or even festive costumes, can make the photos feel more cohesive and memorable. You may include props like oversized candy canes, or wrapped presents to add extra holiday flair. For the backdrop, you can use a decorated Christmas tree, a fireplace with stockings, or even create a DIY snow scene.

Make it a moment filled with laughter by incorporating silly poses. Don't forget to include pets if you have them.

And for those who want a polished look, you can hire a professional photographer or use a tripod and self-timer to capture the perfect frame.

Have fun with the photoshoot.

Eighty Seven

Host a Secret Santa Exchange

Organize a gift exchange with friends, coworkers, or family to spread joy.

Start by setting a budget so everyone feels comfortable and included. Then, draw names. Encourage participants to think creatively about their gift, perhaps choosing something meaningful, funny, or tailored to the recipient's personality.

To add an extra layer of excitement, include hints or clues about the giver in the wrapping or attach a note.

Eighty Eight

Music and Dance

Music and dance have a unique way of lifting spirits and bringing people together. Organize a family or friends dance-off where everyone can show off their best moves.

Play upbeat holiday songs or revisit classic tracks that get everyone on their feet.

To make it even more festive, set up a mini karaoke session where you and your loved ones can belt out your favorite tunes. You could even make it a friendly competition by awarding fun prizes for the most creative dance moves or the best vocal performance.

I tried this during a holiday celebration with my brother. We had the best time singing and dancing to the Madagascar theme song.

Eighty Nine

Cook and Bake

Cooking and baking during the holidays can be a wonderful way to generate joy and create memories.

Gather your family or friends in the kitchen and pick a holiday recipe everyone loves. You can even try something new together.

Ninety

Visit or Connect with Friends and Family

Reconnect with those you care about, especially friends or family members who may feel lonely.

Arrange a visit to an old friend, whether it's to catch up or reminisce about the past.

For family members who may not live nearby, consider video calls or phone check-ins to share updates and laughter.

Small gestures, like showing up with a homemade gift or simply spending quality time together, can mean the world to someone who feels isolated.

Also, you can incorporate some games during your in-person visit.

Board games like Monopoly, Scrabble, or Oware can spark friendly competition and laughter. Additionally, a card game like Uno is easy to play and fun for all ages.

For larger groups, consider party games like Charades, Pictionary, or trivia challenges that get everyone involved and energized.

If you prefer something more active, outdoor games like cornhole, frisbee, soccer, or basketball can be fun.

GRATITUDE

As a part of our daily routines, it's good to reflect on our blessings around us. To wake up in the morning, to be able to breathe, to have a meal, the sound of laughter, a kind word from a stranger, the little things…

Sometimes, it's easy to overlook our blessings, but taking a moment to appreciate them can bring us joy.

Expressing appreciation doesn't have to be elaborate. It's the sincerity behind the gesture that truly matters. By fostering gratitude during the holidays, we'll not only uplift those around us but also nurture a sense of fulfillment and happiness in our own hearts.

Here are a few ways to express gratitude.

Ninety One

Write Thank-You Notes

Take the time to write handwritten thank-you notes for gifts you've received or to show appreciation for someone's kindness or support.

A thoughtful thank-you note doesn't need to be long or overly elaborate. A few heartfelt sentences can go a long way in making someone feel valued.

Mention specific details, such as the gift they gave or the kind gesture they extended, and express how it made you feel.

Ninety Two

Give Compliments

It doesn't take much to brighten someone's day with a kind word or acknowledgment of their hard work. For instance, if someone went out of their way to cook a delicious meal, don't just enjoy it silently. Tell them how much you appreciate their effort and how wonderful the food tastes.

Likewise, notice the small details, like creative holiday decorations or thoughtful acts of kindness, and share your admiration openly.

Don't forget to compliment your friend if you admire their outfit or style.

Even complimenting someone for simply being there for you can make a huge impact.

Ninety Three

Pay It Forward

Paying it forward is a simple yet powerful concept of spreading kindness and gratitude by doing something thoughtful for someone else, often without expecting anything in return. The idea is that one good deed can inspire a chain reaction of generosity.

For example, covering someone's drink or meal, or surprising a neighbor with baked treats can help in spreading holiday cheer.

You could also leave an encouraging note for a colleague, friend, or even a stranger to brighten their day.

Donating gently used clothing, toys, or books to local shelters or charities to help those in need during the season is another way to pay it forward.

Helping a friend or volunteering your time at a community kitchen, food bank, or other local organization is a good way to give back to others during the holidays.

Ninety Four

Create a Gratitude Tree

Have your friends or family members write something they're grateful for on paper ornaments and hang them on a small tree or branch.

I recently saw a Thanksgiving gratitude tree at a friend's house, and it was such a heartwarming idea. She had decorated her tree with notes thanking family members who had supported or helped her throughout the year. It was a simple yet powerful way to show appreciation.

Another friend took a similar approach with her Christmas tree, adorning it with ornaments dedicated to role models who had stood in the gap for her family.

Seeing these creative expressions of gratitude reminded me how important it is to acknowledge the individuals who make a difference in our lives, especially during the holiday season.

Ninety Five

Keep a Gratitude Journal

Keeping a gratitude journal is a simple yet powerful way to focus on the good in your life. Each day, take a few minutes to jot down three things you're thankful for. These could be big moments, like reconnecting with a loved one, or small, everyday joys, like watching a holiday movie.

By reflecting on these positives, your journal becomes a collection of memories and reminders of the blessings in your life.

It'll be perfect to go back and read your journal when you need a little boost of happiness.

Ninety Six

Show Love

When you love someone, whether it's a family member, a close friend, or a partner, don't hold back in letting them know. Tell them.

A simple "I love you" or "I appreciate you" can mean the world to someone who might not hear it often enough.

But don't stop there. Showing love through actions can speak even louder. Small gestures such as spending quality time together, giving a thoughtful gift, or simply offering a hug can remind someone how much they matter to you.

Life is unpredictable, and none of us know how much time we have with the people we care about.

It's so important to cherish every moment and make it count.

Celebrate the little things, create meaningful memories, and always prioritize the relationships that bring joy and meaning to your life.

Ninety Seven

Say 'Thank You' Often

Express your gratitude out loud to those who've made your day brighter. Say thanks for small acts like holding a door open or making you laugh.

Taking a moment to sincerely say "thank you" can have a bigger impact than you realize. It shows the other person that their efforts are noticed and appreciated.

You can also take it a step further by explaining why you're thankful, like saying, "Thank you for lending me an ear today; it really helped me feel calmer."

Whether it's a friend, family member, coworker, or even a stranger, this small acknowledgment can create a positive ripple effect and brighten their day too.

I'd like to use this opportunity to thank my Mama for always lending me her ear. All the phone calls to ask her for basic recipes, to complain about things that may not be going well in my life, to share my joy…

She's ever ready, patiently listening and offering her love and wisdom. Whether it's guiding me through her favorite meat pie recipe or simply reassuring me when my heart is thumping, her support means the world to me.

Thank you, Maa, for being my constant cheerleader and confidante.

Ninety Eight

Acknowledge the Reason for the Holiday

Holidays are a time to reflect on their deeper meaning and the traditions that bring us together.

Whether it's a spiritual celebration, a cultural event, or simply a time to gather with loved ones, acknowledging the reason for the holiday brings a sense of purpose and connection to the season.

No matter your circumstances, take a moment to be thankful for the opportunity to celebrate, whether it's with family, friends, or even in quiet solitude.

Ninety Nine

Reflect Together

Reminisce. Sharing memorable moments or personal accomplishments with your family or close friends is a fun bond building exercise.

You can take turns at the dinner table to share your favorite memories or gather around for a cozy storytelling session.

Whether it's celebrating small victories, like learning a new skill, or major milestones, like a promotion or graduation, reflecting together creates an opportunity to acknowledge each other's growth and successes.

These conversations could be the motivation you need for your next.

One Hundred

Celebrate

Celebrating holidays allows us to pause and enjoy special moments with our friends and family.

Whether you are gathering around for a holiday feast or spending it quietly, remember to mark the occasion with gratitude.

Holidays often bring traditions that connect us to our roots, give us stories to share, and moments to remember.

Although we may not always be enthusiastic during the holiday season, we should try and adopt a heart of gratitude for our basic needs.

Let's always keep in mind those who may not have the means to celebrate. By spreading kindness and paying acts of goodness forward, we can help bring more joy and smiles to people around the world.

Lastly, as we celebrate, let's slow down and acknowledge the beauty in the present.

My Note to You

We are enough. Each of us, exactly as we are, has a purpose on this earth.

Life is an unpredictable journey, and we are here to make the best of the opportunities that come our way.

Even when the road feels uncertain, if we don't find the opportunities we seek, we can create our own.

I want to take a moment to wish you joy. May your dark days be brightened. I wish you peace, the kind that fills your heart and mind throughout life's ups and downs.

May your holidays be meaningful. May you experience love and laughter.

Your presence in this world makes a difference.

Happy holidays!

20 Different Holidays Around the World and Why We Celebrate Them

Christmas (December 25)

Celebrated in many countries, Christmas marks the birth of Jesus Christ in Christian tradition. It is a time for gathering with loved ones, exchanging gifts, and spreading goodwill.

Diwali

Known as the Festival of Lights, Diwali is celebrated in India and by Hindu communities worldwide. It symbolizes the triumph of light over darkness and good over evil.

Eid al-Fitr

This Muslim holiday marks the end of Ramadan, a month of fasting and reflection. It is a celebration of faith, charity, and community, with feasts and the giving of gifts.

Lunar New Year

Widely celebrated across East and Southeast Asia, the Lunar New Year marks the beginning of a new year in the lunar calendar. It is a time for family reunions, honoring ancestors, and wishing for good fortune in the year ahead.

Thanksgiving (Fourth Thursday of November)

Primarily celebrated in the United States and Canada, Thanksgiving is a day to express gratitude for the harvest and blessings of the year through family gatherings and feasts.

Hanukkah

This eight-day Jewish holiday commemorates the rededication of the Second Temple in Jerusalem and the miracle of the oil that burned for eight days. It is celebrated with menorah lighting, prayers, and traditional foods.

Homowo (Ghana)

Homowo, celebrated by the Ga people of Ghana, is a festival that marks the end of a period of famine in their history. The name "Homowo" translates to "hooting at hunger," symbolizing triumph over adversity. It is a time for feasting, music, and honoring the ancestors, with a special celebratory meal of kpokpoi, a traditional dish made from maize.

Día de los Muertos (Day of the Dead)

Celebrated primarily in Mexico and by Mexican communities worldwide, Día de los Muertos is a beautiful tradition that honors deceased loved ones. Taking place on November 1st and 2nd, this festival is about remembering, celebrating, and staying spiritually connected to ancestors. Families create ofrendas (altars) adorned with photos, candles, marigold flowers, and the favorite foods or belongings of their loved ones. Sweet treats like sugar skulls and pan de muerto are also enjoyed. It's not a somber event but rather a vibrant celebration of life and memory, reminding us to cherish and value those who came before us.

Holi

Celebrated in India and Nepal, Holi, the Festival of Colors, signifies the arrival of spring and the victory of good over evil. It is a joyous occasion filled with music, dancing, and vibrant color powders.

Umkhosi Womhlanga (Zulu Reed Dance - South Africa)

This is a traditional Zulu festival in South Africa where young women perform a colorful reed dance to celebrate their culture and purity. It is a joyous occasion that also serves to highlight the value of preserving indigenous traditions and passing them to future generations.

Bastille Day (July 14)

France's National Day commemorates the storming of the Bastille in 1789, a key event in the French Revolution. Celebrations often include parades, fireworks, and communal festivities.

Carnaval

Carnaval is a lively and colorful festival celebrated in many Latin American countries, with some of the most famous celebrations taking place in Brazil, Colombia, and the Dominican Republic. Typically held in the days leading up to Lent, Carnaval is a time of joy, music, and dancing that brings communities together. The festival features parades, elaborate costumes, and traditional music, such as samba in Brazil. It allows people to connect with their cultural heritage while enjoying moments of pure celebration before the observance of Lent. The spirit of Carnaval is all about unity, creativity, and reveling in the vibrancy of life.

Eyo Festival (Nigeria)

The Eyo Festival takes place in Lagos, Nigeria, and is rooted in the cultural traditions of the Yoruba people. This vibrant masquerade festival serves as a tribute to departed ancestors, showcases the cultural heritage of Lagos, and promotes unity within the community. It is marked by colorful processions and the striking imagery of the Eyo masquerades.

Chinese Mid-Autumn Festival

This festival celebrates family unity and the harvest moon. It is honored with mooncakes, lantern lighting, and gatherings under the moonlit sky.

Odwira Festival (Ghana)

Odwira is a sacred festival observed by the Akan people, particularly the Akropong-Akuapem community in Ghana. It is a period of purification, spiritual renewal, and thanksgiving. The festival also celebrates unity among the people and honors deities and ancestors for protection and blessings.

Kwanzaa

A week-long celebration starting on December 26, Kwanzaa honors African American culture and heritage. It focuses on principles like unity, self-determination, and cooperative economics.

Inkaba Yomhlaba (First Fruits Festival - Southern Africa)

Celebrated by the Nguni-speaking communities, this festival honors the land's fertility and abundance. It marks the harvesting season and thanks the ancestors for providing food and prosperity. Rituals, songs, and dances feature prominently during this time.

Indigenous Peoples' Day

Celebrated on the second Monday of October in many places, this day honors the history, culture, and contributions of Native American and Indigenous peoples. It serves as a moment to reflect on the resilience and rich heritage of Native communities while recognizing their lasting impact.

Juneteenth

Celebrated on June 19th, Juneteenth commemorates the emancipation of enslaved

African Americans in the United States. It marks the day in 1865 when the news of the abolishment of slavery reached Texas, two years after the signing of the Emancipation Proclamation. This day is a celebration of freedom, resilience, and African American culture.

New Year's Day

Celebrating New Year's Day is a tradition rooted in history, symbolizing new beginnings and fresh opportunities. Across cultures, it marks the end of one year and the start of another, offering an ideal moment for reflection, gratitude, and goal-setting. It's a global event filled with customs like fireworks, parties, and resolutions. This celebration allows us to come together, bid farewell to the past, and greet the future with optimism and accountability.

References

1. Christmas (December 25): "History of Christmas Traditions and Their Meaning," History.com, A&E Television Networks, https://www.history.com/topics/christmas/history-of-christmas.
2. Diwali: "What Is Diwali? Significance and Celebrations," National Geographic, https://www.nationalgeographic.com/culture/article/diwali.
3. Eid al-Fitr: "Eid al-Fitr," Encyclopaedia Britannica, https://www.britannica.com/topic/Eid-al-Fitr.
4. Lunar New Year: "Lunar New Year 2023," National Geographic Kids, https://kids.nationalgeographic.com/celebrations/article/chinese-new-year.
5. Thanksgiving (Fourth Thursday of November): "The History of Thanksgiving," Smithsonian Magazine, https://www.smithsonianmag.com.
6. Hanukkah: "Hanukkah," My Jewish Learning,

https://www.myjewishlearning.com/articl
e/hanukkah-101.

7. Homowo (Ghana): "Homowo Festival,"
   Ghana Tourism Authority,
   [http://visitghana.com](http://visitghana.c
   om).

8. Día de los Muertos (Day of the Dead):
   "Day of the Dead," Smithsonian Latino
   Center,
   [https://latino.si.edu/DayOfTheDead](htt
   ps://latino.si.edu/DayOfTheDead).

9. Holi Festival: "Festival of Colors," Holi
   Festival Organization,
   https://www.holifestival.org.

10. Umkhosi Womhlanga (Zulu Reed
    Dance): "Umkhosi Womhlanga," South
    Africa Tourism,
    [https://www.southafrica.net](https://ww
    w.southafrica.net).

11. Bastille Day (July 14): "Bastille Day in
    France," France.fr,
    [https://www.france.fr](https://www.franc
    e.fr).

12. Carnaval: "Carnival History and
    Traditions," Brazil Tourism Board,
    https://www.visitbrasil.com.

13. Eyo Festival (Nigeria): "Eyo Festival of
    Lagos," The Guardian Nigeria,

https://guardian.ng
.

14. Chinese Mid-Autumn Festival: "Mid-Autumn Festival," Time Out Shanghai, https://www.timeoutshanghai.com.
15. Odwira Festival (Ghana): "Cultural Festivals – Odwira," Ghana Web, https://www.ghanaweb.com.
16. Kwanzaa: "Kwanzaa History and Traditions," Official Kwanzaa Website, https://www.officialkwanzaawebsite.org.
17. Inkaba Yomhlaba (First Fruits Festival - Southern Africa): "Nguni First Fruits Tradition," South African Heritage Foundation, https://www.nih.ms.gov.za.
18. Indigenous Peoples' Day: "Honoring Indigenous Peoples' Day," Smithsonian National Museum of the American Indian, https://americanindian.si.edu.
19. Juneteenth: "The Historical Legacy of Juneteenth," National Museum of African American History and Culture, https://nmaahc.si.edu.

20. New Year's Day: "New Year Traditions Around the World," BBC News, https://www.bbc.com.

Acknowledgements

To my family, thank you for your unwavering love and support during both the joyful and challenging moments of the holidays. Your kindness, patience, and sense of togetherness remind me of what truly matters.

To my friends, your encouragement and shared experiences have given me the courage to open up and share the ups and downs of this season.

Each of you has played a special role in shaping my perspective, and for that, I will always be grateful. Thank you for being part of this special journey.

About the Author

Harper Carr is a storyteller who likes to inspire and connect with readers. With a background rooted in community engagement, Harper believes in the power of storytelling to spark meaningful conversations. Drawing on personal experiences and a love for diverse cultures, Harper writes from the heart. Whether writing fiction or nonfiction, she hopes to have a positive impact on her readers.

Dear Reader

If you enjoyed reading this book, I would greatly appreciate it if you could take a moment to leave a review and share it with others. I hope that our "100 Ways of Celebrating Holidays" inspires you to spread joy, create wonderful memories, and bring positive energy to yourself and your loved ones. Thank you for your support.

Stronger Together,

Harper

www.ingramcontent.com/pod-product-compliance
Lightning Source LLC
Chambersburg PA
CBHW060325050426
42449CB00011B/2651